TOTAL RECALL

REMEMBERING THE
ORIGINAL YOU

By Michael A. Danforth

Acknowledgments

Cover graphic Image used by permission. All rights reserved.

All interior images are given by permission and licensed through www.Fotolia.com

Io9.com George Dvorsky/ Neuroscience /Meditation

ISBN 978-0981594477

September 2013

Printed in the United States of America

Total Recall - Remembering The Original You

© MTI Publishing 2013 by Michael A. Danforth, Yakima, Washington

MTI
PO Box 43 Yakima, WA 98907
www.mticenter.com

Editing and page layout by
Michael and Melanie Murphy/
Arlene Baldwin

Referenced Quotes:

Neal M.D., Mary C. "To Heaven and Back"
Robin Sharma "The Leader Who Had No Title"
Wikipedia free encyclopedia "wikipedia.org"

Table of Contents

4

INTRODUCTION

Before we enter into this journey of recalling forgotten information or experiences prior to our earthly state, let me quickly clear the table in regards to other religious organizations that have taught or believe in a preexistent form of spirit prior to physical birth. While some spiritual organizations might bear witness to what I write in this book, I am by no means intentionally supporting any particular religious group or view on this matter. I am simply revealing what I believe the Lord has shown me about our previous origin of existence and the importance of recalling the necessary parts that are important to our intended purpose in Him.

In addition, I realize how tempting it can be to manipulate scripture and interpret it to fit our particular point of view.

Therefore, even though I have discovered many other scriptures that seem to shed light on the possibility of our previous state as spiritual beings, I chose not to refer to them due to the shallowness of their foundational support. Even though some might disagree with the resources I have compiled together in this book, they are nonetheless gathered with the upmost intent to equip the people of God toward spiritual maturity. So let the journey begin.

The ability to recall or remember is a daily part of our lives. Without memory, you would not be able to perform the basic functions of life. Think about it. As soon as you wake from a night of sleep, the first thing you do is remember what you were doing before you closed your eyes and what you have to do next. Whether you are at work, driving down the road, planning your next steps, whatever the situation might be, you are constantly in the mode of having to remember something.

Without the basic usage of memory, you wouldn't be able to dialogue with a friend or co-worker. The ability to recall or remember something is one of the main ingredients of our human existence. Literally, life as we know it today would not exist. If it were not for the power of "recall," I wouldn't be able to write this book.

Recall, is defined as, *"Bringing a fact, event, or situation into one's mind, especially for the purpose of recounting it to others."* It is the act of returning to a particular place and time in one's mind.

Remember, is defined as, *"The act of being able to bring to one's mind an awareness of someone or something that one has seen, known, or experienced in the past."*

As you can see, recall and remember are very much alike in meaning. Throughout this book, I will be using both words interchangeably.

For the most part, our range of recall has always been within the borders of our earliest childhood up to recent years, months, days, hours, etc... However, what if we could recall something that was pre-earth? What if our ability to remember exceeded any earthly experience we have ever had? What if we could recall some forgotten information that was given to us prior to our earthly conception? The question that should be asked is not whether we had knowledge of our lives prior to becoming flesh, but rather, why can't we remember? If indeed we did exist on some spiritual plane before time, then why can't we recall or remember any of the details?

Some believe we were just a form of energy floating around waiting to take on earthly form.

Others believe any memories of our previous spiritual state were wiped clean like the hard drive of a computer before entering into the human race. It's certainly plausible, but I do not believe that this is the case.

First, I would like to suggest that everyone, at one point or another in life, has experienced a measure of recall that is beyond any human experience. There are countless moments when we discover new things about ourselves for the very first time. However, there are other times when we are actually remembering something that we experienced prior to being born in the earth.

These moments of self-revelation are the act of recall. It's the resurfacing of knowledge that was given to us in our former state of glory. It takes both the spirit and the natural to initiate memory. Having a personal relationship with Jesus is not a requirement for walking in recollective awareness. Millions of people in the world today, who have not established a personal connection with God, are currently walking in the purpose of God for their lives at one level or another. My point is, the Spirit of God can still lead and direct people in multiple areas of their life without them being fully aware that it is God doing it. Of course, there are tremendous benefits to having an intimate relationship with the Spirit of God and certainly necessary before one is able to see his/her life from a divine perspective.

Our exposures to all the early facets of life, from the moment we are in the womb, to our hour of death, have the potential to enhance or hinder our recollection of God's plans for our life.

THE CALL TO REMEMBER

Throughout the world, there is an echoing call to remember. Remembering is an important practice throughout biblical scripture. There are multiple scriptures instructing the people of God to remember important events and teachings that were pertinent to their spiritual advancement.

"Remember the Sabbath day, to keep it holy. (Ex 2:8)

"Remember Abraham, Isaac and Israel..." (Ex 32:13)

"Remember the days of old..."(Dt 32:7)

Isaiah writes,

"Do not remember the former things, nor consider the things of old. (Isa 43:18)

In one instance, the people of God are instructed to remember the past, and then in another, they are told to forget it. This implies there are some things in the past that are worthy of remembering, while many other things are not.

Other biblical references describe our need for wanting God to recall or bring to mind former promises.

Remember, Lord, your loving kindness and tender mercies...Ps 25:6

Remember, Lord, the reproach of your servants... (Ps 89:50)

God even invites Israel to remind Him of His promises toward them.

"Put Me in remembrance, let us argue our case together; State your *cause*, that you may be proved right." (Isaiah 43:26)

Seriously, the list of "remembrance" is seemingly endless. Without the power of recall, or memory, our spiritual maturation would be impossible.

For the most part, we have been taught that our purpose and destiny in life is out there somewhere in front of us. I would agree that this is the case in terms of wanting to see the intent of God for our lives tangibly appear. However, *I believe the timing of those same plans becoming visible can be hindered by our methods of discovery.*

As I indicated before, there are some things worth recalling and there are other things worth forgetting. It's certainly no secret that most people struggle in the area of wanting to know their purpose in life.

The idea behind *"total recall"* is not just about breaking the barrier of remembrance, thus discovering the initial plans of God, but it is also about overriding any unpleasant memory that has kept His glorious purposes from surfacing into the conscious reality of one's soul.

While the future ahead of us is something we have to sort out along the way, I believe this divine sorting is reliant upon our ability to recall the intent of heaven for our lives.

I think I can offer you a strong case as to why the plans of God for our lives were instigated before time. I am equally convinced that we were given the opportunity to discuss and view those plans in advance. It is my hope not only to convince you of your prior involvement in God's original function and purpose for your life, but to help you and encourage you to recall that same divine knowledge. As already stated, I'm not implying that every detail of our journey has been preplanned, but that the **overall** plan or function for our life has been predetermined before the foundations of the world. I am also not implying that the initial plan of God for our lives is set on some sort of autopilot. Even though the plans of eternity are within each of us, it still requires personal surrender and cooperation.

THE TREASURE IS IN YOU

One of the advantages that we all have is that the plans of God for our lives, like a hidden treasure, are locked away inside our spiritual DNA.

"This treasure is in earthen vessels..." (2Cor 4:7)

Our eternal future is already in us. God has given us the necessary keys to unlock the full value of His glorious intent toward us. From the beginning, amazing treasures of endless possibilities have been placed within each of us.

This means, *what now appears to be in front of you, is in you and what is in you was given to you before time.* Like Jesus, we carry specific instructions for our lives in advance.

Our present journey is not so much about getting a new plan from God as it is about discovering the plan that God gave to us long before our natural birth. Again, our journey includes the collective wisdom and understanding as to how we are to carry out those plans. This means there are details within our journey that are a day-to-day process of making choices, praying for wisdom and understanding, all the while recognizing those things that are linked to the advancement of God's kingdom in us.

This does not mean that the bigger picture for our lives is only about one thing, one subject, or one function. In the beginning, the plan of God can look like one thing, but eventually turn into something quite different from what you had known before. Many of you already know what that is like. Your life started out looking like one thing, but then shifted into something much different. The result can become quite colorful.

Let there be no doubt, we are destined for greatness not because we will become great, but because we are already great. We are the seed of our Father, reconciled by the death and resurrection of Jesus Christ. Even before Christ, there were those like Jeremiah and John the Baptist, who were given the opportunity to recall their former state of glory, thus their intended purpose in the kingdom of God. Yet now today, we who are in Christ are empowered by the Holy Spirit to regain forgotten knowledge that pertains to our journey here on earth. Therefore, it is my prayer for you, that like Jesus, you will recall your former state of glory, thus influencing the world in ways unimaginable.

One last note:

In this book I will intentionally repeat myself, while phrasing it slightly differently each time: not for the purpose of adding more pages, but to take you deeper into a greater understanding of the subject at hand, which is purposed to help you remember the real you, the spirit you, as well as the plans of God for your life.

I'M BEGINNING TO REMEMBER

One day I was speaking at a conference in southern Idaho, when all of a sudden I entered into an intense realm of knowledge; a realm of wisdom that was beyond my field of study. Like a raging river, the revelation of heaven flowed through me. I begin to describe things about my life, things I didn't even know that I knew about myself. I started describing other things, creatures, sounds and colors, all of which seemed very familiar to me.

During this intense revelatory moment, I told the people,

"I know this is going to sound strange, but everything I just told you, I have always known. I have already experienced. I'm not sure how, but I have always known these things. They have

always been in me. It's as if I am just now remembering them."

This was my initiation of realizing my ability to recall former knowledge, before time. Since then I have been in the process of total recall. There were moments in my adolescent years when I thought about things that felt extremely real, but incomprehensible. I know now that it was the Holy Spirit at work. It was like flashbacks of moments that were totally disconnected with any earthly experience. I have since remembered eternal assignments that were given to me before arriving on planet earth. Walking those assignments out has been a daily process in my life. I know this sounds like some sci-fi moment, but the lack of awareness or perception, is the primary reason most of the plans of God for our lives are overlooked.

The fact is, many of you reading this have had some moments of supernatural déjà vu.

Judith Orloff, M.D., is an Assistant Clinical Professor of Psychiatry at UCLA and the author of *Emotional Freedom.*

Concerning Déjà vu, she writes,

"Déjà Vu" is a common intuitive experience that has happened to many of us. The expression is derived from the French, meaning, "already seen." When it occurs, it seems to spark our memory of a place we have already been, a person we have already seen, or an act we have already done. It is a signal to pay special attention to what is taking place, perhaps to receive a specific lesson in a certain area or complete what is not yet finished."

When I came across this description of Déjà vu, I thought, *"That is exactly what is happening. It is a moment of a receptive awareness that, for a brief moment, enables us to recall information that is in some way pertinent to our spiritual journey on earth."*

Of course, much of the scientific world explains déjà vu encounters as being nothing more than pre-stored information in the brain, which when encountering a similar experience in the future, brings that previous information to mind. However, there are an equal number of physicists who do not deny the fact that the source of this information could come from outside the natural realm.

I think one of the key words is "perception." When you have that sensation of "I have seen or heard this before", perceive in that moment the possibility that what you are experiencing is indeed the spirit encouraging you to remember a piece of God's plan for your life.

Right now, I want to stir you to remembrance. I want to stir your spirit to recall the essence of those previous moments of glory right now. Let me say, with all boldness and confidence, you <u>can</u>, and you <u>will</u>, because they are still in you. Like the words of Jesus, "they are life, they are spirit."

Ok. Let's do a little exercise right now. Just read this aloud.

"Holy Spirit, thank You for bringing to my remembrance everything that I have ever encountered in God, which includes everything before time. Thank You for giving me total recall of the plan of Father for my life."

We will be repeating these "recall" exercises throughout this book. In return, you will discover how ***a simple step of faith can lead you into a sudden moment of total recall.***

The more you dial your spiritual senses into a cognitive state, the more you will be able to distinguish the difference between new revelations, which is hearing something for the first time, versus recalling something that was already in you, but forgotten.

I need to say this again: everyone has a measure of former knowledge in them; you just lack the memory of it. The reason it's so easily overlooked is that there is no reference point, no touching post of understanding to make you aware that what you are seeing or experiencing is indeed a moment of supernatural recall. Right now, the touching point for total recall is spirit, engaging, interacting and dialoguing with the Spirit.

You mark these words; as I have already stated, *"A time is coming when this understanding will spread like a raging fire. Special moments of recall will serve as a tool to navigate countless people out of the darkness of earthly memories that have tormented them for years."*

Even when I was walking through some of the darkest and rebellious years of my life, there were moments when I was arrested by an acute knowledge of supernatural recall, or an awareness of my true intended state in God. I would get glimpses of God's divine plan for my life. I somehow knew in my heart that it was pre-earth; that it was knowledge from before the foundations of the world.

I am so thankful that the Holy Spirit is a multitasker. It seems He can achieve more in a single moment of time than all my accumulated times put together. I am so thankful that He is continually working in my life. He is the power of advancement within me; within all of us. One of His assignments is to help us remember the anointed appointments for our lives.

"But the Helper, the Holy Spirit, whom the Father will send in My name, He will teach you all things, and bring to your remembrance all that I said to you." (John 14:26)

Each of us is blessed to have the Holy Spirit teaching us every step of the way. He was given to us to teach us *all things*, not just the things that Jesus taught while on earth, but everything that pertains to life.

Are you hearing this? The Holy Spirit is with us to bring to our remembrance everything Jesus discussed not only in His day, while He was living on earth, but everything else that was spoken to us prior to this time. He is the remembering force working in our lives whether we are awake or asleep. Some of my greatest moments of recalling kingdom knowledge have occurred when I was sleeping.

I don't know how many times when I have awakened the next day only to realize that the Spirit had visited me in my dreams, equipping me and teaching me how to live as a true son of God here on planet earth. Think about this. The

Holy Spirit was there when your future on earth was being planned. He is indeed our divine counselor. He is our source of comfort at any given moment. In addition, one of His objectives is to bring to our remembrance all things, past, present and future.

REMEMBERING THROUGH WORSHIP

I have always been partial to king David and his gift as a psalmist. His spontaneous interaction with everyday life and the glory of the Lord has always inspired me to spontaneously engage with the Lord through praise and worship. For years, my gift as a spiritual psalmist in the kingdom of God has literally unveiled the glory of heaven in me. Like David, through worship I have encountered the mysteries and pathways of God. Many of my moments of recall have come through these special moments of worship.

Few people realize that David had moments of "recall" multiple times over. One of the amazing things about biblical scripture, for the most part, you can find evidence that relates to every spiritual encounter you have ever had in God.

This is not to say that every genuine encounter with God is spelled out in the Bible. If that were the case, then the extent of God would be limited to recorded scripture, which means He would have a beginning and an end. Nonetheless, the bible is loaded with an endless stream of kingdom revelation.

However, any real encounter with God will never contradict biblical scripture. It is understood that the bible is subject to interpretation. Most people have difficulty seeing truth outside the framework of their current state of understanding. It used to be that one of my greatest challenges was seeing beyond my former biblical training. Don't get me wrong, I am still very challenged at various levels of scriptural understanding, but certainly far less than before.

One of the primary keys to seeing outside the box of present understanding is conditioning yourself to do so. I'm not saying you need to abandon every former truth, but you must be willing to look beyond what you already perceived to be true.

Many have yet to discover that we actually see with our mind, not with our eyes. In other words, whatever perceived image you have in your mind in the moment, is often our present window of sight.

One day I was home looking for a bottle of vitamin B12. My wife Lori told me that it was in the hallway closet on the second shelf. In my mind, the color of the bottle I was looking for was blue, because that was the color of the previous bottle I had used. So I scanned over every bottle on the first, second and third shelf. No B12.

Feeling a bit agitated I said, "Lori I can't find it anywhere and I've looked on every shelf." She responds, "Really? Why is it you can never find these things and I can?" (I'm sure you've never heard those words before) I replied, "I'm telling you, there is no B12 in this closet."

Lori comes to where I am at, looks in the closet and in a matter of seconds, pulls out, not one, but two green bottles of B12. I will leave her last reply to your imagination.

You see, I was looking for a blue bottle of B12, not a green one. Even though there were two bottles right in front of me clearly marked "B12" I could not see beyond the image in my own mind.

This is the challenging sight of knowledge. It can either reveal things that are hidden or blind us to the obvious reality that is right in front of us. I want to suggest to you that if you are still having difficulty seeing the possibility of engaging with the Lord prior to your earthly form, thus gaining memory of those times, then maybe, just maybe, your looking for a blue bottle instead of a green one.

David writes,

"Your eyes have seen my unformed substance; and in Your book were all written the days that were ordained for me, when as yet there was not one of them." (Psalms 139:16)

I love this! David obviously had an eye-opening encounter worshipping God. One that brought him into the realization that God knew him before he became flesh and blood.

He also discovered a book where all the ordained days of his life were recorded. These same prerecorded days were just waiting to be fulfilled in David's life. This is why I have repeatedly said,

"The present and future on earth, is the past in heaven!" Come on God!

This is the image you need to see in your heart and mind right know. A book. A book of records. One that has record of all the ordained purposes for your life. If you can see this, then you are at the gate of discovering the future intentions of God. This word "book" is the Hebrew word *"say-fer"* which means *ciphrah or cipher.* It implies secret writings or coded text. This book or personal scroll for your life is written in code; Holy Spirit code, and only the Spirit of God can reveal its meaning.

I have seen the book/scroll of records for my life. Though I have not seen all that it contains, I am committed to discovering more every day. Even more incredible, Holy Spirit is far more determined to help me gain knowledge of all the recorded intent of heaven for me, thus bringing me into remembrance of my purposed quest on earth and in heaven.

One of my recent experiences with the scroll of records gave me an increasing revelation of the mountain of the Lord. In fact, on this same mountain, through the psalmist anointing in my life, I have long had the opportunity to look into the future, to see into other worlds, to make decrees, as well as, recall several encounters of my previous glorious state in God.

During this recent encounter, like so many times before, I was worshiping with great intent. I often worship by myself in the privacy of my home, but this time Lori was with me. The realm of glory became so intense that the Lord began to sing to me, through me. While this is often a common occurrence for me, this time, I was carried away into memorial moment in the Spirit.

As the Lord continued to sing to me, through me, He directed my attention toward a mountain. When I looked toward the mountain, I could see myself standing on top of it worshiping the Lord.

He then said to me, *"See that mountain? You asked if you could worship and reign on that mountain and I said, "Yes." Therefore, I gave you that mountain. It is a mountain of worship, one of reigning glory. It is your mountain."*

Suddenly, I was on the mountain, seemingly in real time, worshiping God. As I looked from the mountain, I had a panoramic view of the New Jerusalem. As I continued to worship, I could see people coming from the great city of the Lord, climbing the mountain He had given to me.

I then turned and saw the psalmist David standing beside me worshiping God. This was when I realized that it wasn't my voice drawing them to the mountain, but the voice of the Lord. Remember? The Lord was singing to me, through me. They knew His sound. What was even more exciting was that Lori was able to experience this mountain for herself, through the song of the Lord. It was a glorious bonding moment for the both of us. :-)

Though I have spiritually occupied this mountain for a number of years, I had no memory of asking the Lord to give me that mountain until now. What a wonderful encounter. What an amazing moment of total recall. Come on God!

I must prophesy to you now.

"When this generation hears the sound of heaven coming from the mountains of the Lord, in the New Jerusalem, they will climb their mountain and worship Him. For in this New Jerusalem, in the Holy City of God, there are many mountains waiting to be discovered for such a time as this."

"Now it shall come to pass in the latter days

That the mountain of the LORD's house

Shall be established on the top of the mountains,

And shall be exalted above the hills;

And peoples shall flow to it.

Many nations shall come and say,

"Come, and let us go up to the mountain of the LORD..." (Micah 4:1-2)

PAST, PRESENT AND FUTURE

From a kingdom standpoint, the future isn't just from the future; it's from the past as well. The future is mixed with new revelation and experiences, as well as former revelation and experiences. All of which are in the present with us now.

In heaven, the past, present and future, occupy the same space at the same time. Heaven is not dimensional in terms of time as it is on earth.

The concept of "the future" is based on something that is present, yet invisible, but expected to become visible at another point in time.

Therefore, when speaking about the future, we are talking about events and things that have not yet appeared in their visible form, but presently exist in the eternal realms of God's kingdom.

Just because something is not visible doesn't mean it's not already here. There is a "heavenly present" and an "earthly present." In terms of visibility, what is visibly present in heaven is not necessarily visibly present on earth. Therefore, we cannot make the assumption that what we cannot see with our eyes is not already here.

Jesus instructed his disciples to pray,

"Your kingdom come, Your will be done, on earth as it is in heaven." (Matthew 6:10)

This means there are things presently in heaven that need to become visible on earth. It also means that just as there is a will of God for heaven so there is a will God for earth.

Speaking of Abraham, "...*even* God, who gives life to the dead and calls into being that which does not exist." (Romans 4:17)

It literally means, "Call the things which do not exist that do exist in another realm."

In other words, speak to them as if they are already here.

This is how we are to view purpose and destiny. It already exists in another realm; we just need to call it into present day reality.

This should come as no shock because it is no different than seeing the gift of healing at work or anything else that pertains to the supernatural. When we pray for someone to be healed, we do so with the understanding that "by His stripes we are healed." (Isaiah 53:5) Past tense.

The object of the prayer is an action to manifest what already exists in heaven into the earth. The point being, you are establishing something that has already been established in heaven, but not on earth.

In respect to the election of God for your life, let me be so bold as to say it like this, *"the other you, the spirit you, was declared fully functional in another realm, before this present time"*.

To the degree that we are able to recall the plan of God, is the degree that we will take on the mind of that plan here and now.

In many ways, discovery is as much about remembering what you once knew, as it is about discovering something new. Sometimes, in respect to knowledge, what appears to be new is really something old. It is something foreknown.

The Hebrew word for "tomorrow" is "mahhar" which comes from the root word "ahhar" which means, **"to be behind."**

The Hebrew word for yesterday is "temel" which comes from the root word "mul" which means **"in front of."**

From a Hebraic perspective, what is visible is "in front of" and what is invisible "is behind." In this sense, the past is the future and the future is the past. Yes, I know, it is somewhat of a mind twister. It's like saying what is upside down is really right side up. In terms of the future, whatever becomes visible on earth today was already visible in another realm. Therefore, what we consider the future on earth is actually the past in heaven. This is not to say that everything that occurs on earth has already occurred in heaven in the sense of physical manifestation.

Many things that happen on planet earth are simply a daily by-product of right or wrong choices. This means restoration is needed to bring the people of God back into alignment with the original design of heaven. However, it does not mean that we are not still moving forward, it just means, sometimes, like in the days of Moses, you might have to go the long way around to get to the nearest place.

If you consider yourself to be prophetic in the sense of knowing the future, then you have to become acquainted with what is already in heaven, because the future here, is the past there.

When Moses asked the Lord to show him His glory, the Lord responded with these words.

"You cannot see My face, for no man can see Me and live!" Then the LORD said, "Behold, there is a place with Me, and you shall stand *there* on the rock; and it will come about, while My glory is passing by, that I will put you in the cleft of the rock and cover you with My hand until I have passed by. Then I will take My hand away and you shall see My back, but My face shall not be seen." (Exodus 33:20-23)

The Hebrew word "face" is "pawneem" which comes from the root word "pawnaw" which means "in front of or before." It carries the meaning of, "before time." God was telling Moses, to see My face is to see before time.

This means the face of God's glory is where He has already been. Therefore, the back of God's glory is our future. When Moses saw the backside of God, he saw future generations rising up in the power and glory of Jesus Christ. I believe, from that moment on, Moses led Israel into a place where he had already been in the spirit. Come on God!

Without getting sidetracked let me give you a personal example of something existing in the spirit then becoming visible thereafter.

On September 6, 2009, I was speaking at a Mountain Top gathering in Yakima, WA. During that meeting, I was interrupted by a word of knowledge, which is what often happens with me.

I shouted, *"Come on! Come on! The rotation of the earth is beginning to shift; it's shifting on its axis right now. What is this unusual alignment? Even this unusual movement that is taking place in the cosmos right now...?"*

I continued to describe unusual events that were transpiring in space, events that pointed to a spiritual representation of an unusual alignment that was occurring within the body of Christ.

A few months later, on February 27, 2010 Chile experienced an earthquake. A more devastating earthquake had preceded this Chilean earthquake one month prior, shaking the region of Haiti and killing more than 230,000 people. Following the aftermath of the Chilean earthquake, the national media released the following report.

"Chilean Earthquake Altered Earth Axis, Shortening day." (Foxnews.com February 27, 2010)

I assure you, had I known that the shifting of the earth's axis was going to be the aftermath of a horrific event, I would have done some serious intersession in attempt to alter those circumstances.

You see, what I saw in the moment, to me, had already happened. Therefore, from a spiritual perspective, the earth shifting on its axis in the future, for me, was a past event. Many future events that appear to be set in concrete are subject to change. Even the original design of God for our life is subject to change, which often depends upon the choices we make.

I often use the GPS that is on my phone instead of the one that is in the car. Anyone who has ever driven with me knows my amazing ability to miss my turn or get lost while driving. As many of you well know, the wonderful thing about GPS navigation is no matter how many times you miss your turn it will redirect you toward the next correct route.

This is a simple illustration of what it is like for the Spirit of God to navigate us through life. If we miss an important turn, He will patiently guide us to the next turn or exit. My point being, more than one road will lead you to your future destination. God only knows how many times I missed my chance, over and over again, but by the grace and faithfulness of God, I was brought back on course by heaven's divine GPS. Come on God!

PERSONAL PLANNING ANGELS

Recently, I read a book written by Mary C. Neal M.D. entitled *"To Heaven and Back."* In this book, Mary speaks about a kayaking trip she went on in southern Chile.

She describes her capsized kayak pinning her under the surging water. According to her family and kayaking friends who were there at the time, Mary was not breathing for 15 to 25 minutes. During the time of what she terms her "drowning," she claims to have had a heavenly experience in which she returned to God and was in the presence of Jesus and angels.

One of her angelic conversations was about the reasons why we are given the opportunity to come to earth, which you will have to read her book to learn. During this same angelic encounter, Mary speaks about what the Lord told her concerning a time of preparation for our journey to earth.

She writes,

"We are able to make a basic outline for our life. This is not to imply that we, the humans, are entirely in charge of our life's design. It is more like God creates it, then we review it and discuss it with our "personal planning" angel."

While reading this, I remember turning to my wife Lori and shouting, "I knew it! I have known this for a very long time!" I continued, "Remember Lori? Remember all those times when I would be standing before an audience and say, "I don't know how I know this, but I have always known what I am telling you right now."

The fact is, each of us has a planning angel that is, and was, personally involved in the daily affairs of our lives. I am not saying this based on one woman's experience, who, by the way, was once a very skeptical surgeon until this tragic event turned her world upside down, or should I say, right side up.

Much of what I am telling you is based on my own personal knowledge and experience with the predestined plan of God for my life.

When I first experienced the memory of God in my life, it was as though a huge weight was lifted off me. In that moment, life was no longer about me trying to make something happen or devise a plan for my life that was not already set in motion. My ordained journey became much more simplified. Not necessarily easier, but less vague, much clearer, which has afforded me a greater place of peace, rest and kingdom advancement.

Let me insert a very important revelation concerning the plans of God for our lives. While knowing that the plans of God are important, they are secondary to sonship. Sonship is the first and foremost objective of our purpose for living. In one of my books, *"God Wanted a Son"* (which I am presently re-writing) I describe how God always wanted a son; he always wanted sons and daughters. He always wanted to be a Father. *One of the wonderful things about being a father is knowing your children have a future.*

"I know the plans that I have for you,' declares the LORD, 'plans for welfare and not for

calamity to give you a future and a hope."
(Jeremiah 29:11)

The initial plans and purposes are secondary or a by-product of that reality. Therefore, whether sin had become an issue or not, the manifestation of sonship would have still been in motion and the primary focus in God's heart fulfilled. This is really good news because this means that the manifested Son of God was the result of love, not sin. In other words, even if there were no works of the devil to be destroyed, the primary purpose of God was to always have sons/daughters, because he always wanted a family.

Isn't it great to know that the angel(s) Father has assigned to your life are fully aware of your purpose and destiny in Him? Moreover, isn't it just as great to know that you were somehow allowed to interact with your destined journey prior to being born? Come on God!

Therefore, because of the Holy Spirit, our helper, and our wonderful assigned angels, we are not only in the position to discover the needed essentials for our journey, but we are also in the position of recalling certain planned events that took place during our round table experience in heaven.

Right now, in this very moment, I am detecting something very strong in the spirit. I have a strong sense that before you reach the end of this book you are going to have a significant "recall" encounter. You will not only realize the purpose of God for your life, but you will also tap into the secrets of heaven that are inside of you right now. Come on! That's good news!

I am also sensing by the spirit that the forces that have come against you, hoping to discourage you for the sole purpose of derailing the plans of God in you, are losing their grip. Not only are you on the edge of remembering the first eternal ordination of your life, but you are on the brink of discovering what it really means to occupy a human body for the brief privilege of exhibiting the love of God and His supernatural kingdom on earth.

ILLUMINATION

I think that before most people are convinced of the possibility of gaining "total recall" they have to know for sure if they ever existed in some spiritual state prior to their physical form on earth. For some, this requires some real, concrete evidence. Therefore, in conjunction with some excellent personal testimonies that are in this book, we will look more closely at "spirit" and its previous state of glory.

Many believe that when the Spirit of God entered into Adam and Jesus that no one else ever needed to have any kind of individual introduction of Spirit before coming into the earth. Meaning that once Spirit entered into the earth it transfers itself repeatedly from one vessel to the next throughout the ages. Obviously, in respect to Old Testament scripture and the life of Jesus, the way that God chose to manifest His spirit is indeed unique.

There are many examples of how our ancient ancestors transferred blessings from one son to the next, as well as Jesus transferring the same power that was working in Him to others. Even after the ascension of Jesus, we can see the impartation of the Holy Spirit being transferred from one generation to the next.

However, it's important to note that it wasn't because these same people did not have the life of God in them, because they did. After all, without some measure of spirit the physical body would be unsustainable, which leads me to the subject of John, the son of Zachariah and Elizabeth. His birth was without a doubt unique.

"There came a man sent from God, whose name was John. He came as a witness, to testify about the Light, so that all might believe through him. He was not the Light, but *he came* to testify about the Light. There was the true Light which, coming into the world, enlightens every man." (John 1:6-9)

In these few passages, we can clearly see that John was sent from God. This means John was sent for a very specific purpose. He was sent to testify about the Light, Jesus. John was born with an uncanny knowledge of the plan of God for his life.

In verse 9, John states that the purpose of the true Light, Jesus, was to "enlighten" or to give light to every man.

The Greek word for light means to *"illuminate or to make one see."* This tells us that one of the primary objectives of Jesus was to open our eyes. He literally came to 'turn on the lights.' Jesus the Light took us out of a dark place so we could see, so we could remember who we are in God. The light of God doesn't just shine upon our present and future, but He shines on our past as well. He shines on our eternal past, not the past of the flesh, but the past of the spirit. He wants us to see and know who we were, who we are now and who we are destined to be.

Samuel declared,

"For You are my lamp, O LORD;
And the LORD illumines my darkness." (2 Samuel 22:29)

The Hebrew word for *"darkness "is "ignorance, misery, and obscurity."* Jesus came to do away with anything that obscures us from our eternal state in God. *He is the ultimate "ignorance" remover.* He doesn't want us to be ignorant of anything that pertains to life.

There is no doubt in my mind that John knew who he was in the spirit. Imagine appearing in the world knowing that your primary function was to be a testimony of the eternal Light of God.

One of the keys to holding onto eternal memories from an early age, even from birth, is to be in an environment that nurtures the child according to his/her purpose in God. Mind you, even those who are not brought up in a Christ-like environment can still discover the plan of God for their lives. This is part of the preplanning purpose of God. Each individual who is born into the world, when exposed to the right conditions, can take on his/her intended function, whether it is science, finances, education, entertainment etc. Many who are born in less desirable conditions are afforded the same opportunity to know the plan of God for their lives, but the process of getting there might not be as accommodating. However, in the end, the less desirable road has the potential to produce the greatest impact for the kingdom of God.

Unlike some, John was privileged to be born in a very accommodating situation. The conditions were ripe for his earthly entrance. His father's priestly heritage and his mother, who was from the line of Aaron, formed the needed environment for John to be raised. In addition, John's mother and father were keenly aware of his destiny and were equipped to bring him up accordingly.

They knew what it was like to "train up a child in the way he should go, so when he is old he will not depart from it." **(Proverbs 22:6)**

This thinking can cause one to look at this passage of scripture in an entirely new light. Having revelation of your children's purpose enhances their ability to rise up into their intended function in God much more quickly, as well as increasing their capability to recall any and every former engagement of the spirit.

Imagine what would happen if millions of children were guarded and nurtured according to the plan of God for their lives. The impact of the kingdom of God upon the earth would be far more staggering than it is today. The senseless deaths of children of all ages over the last several years has been heart wrenching. Yet, you can be assured that their deaths will not go unchecked. You can be equally assured that the future births of boys and girls will carry in them the revelation of heaven exponentially, thus the vengeance of their Father against every work of the enemy.

As stated earlier, God sent John into the world to fulfill a certain task. You don't send someone on a mission without first making sure those plans are somehow protected and embedded in his/her spiritual makeup one way or another. As just mentioned, even if a child is not brought up in the right environment, there are still ways to ensure that the plans of God are progressively triggered by the circumstances of life. Therefore, destiny is about discovering and remembering.

God is the master planner. He is the master builder. He has been around the block once or twice. He knows how to get it done.

History proves that God is a God of design. God created the world by design. This means He created with purpose. It means God already had something in mind before things were put into motion. From Adam to Noah, all the way to Jesus, God made clear His intentions and exercised whatever means necessary to carry them out.

John the Baptist was no exception. Thus, the strict guidelines given to Zachariah and Elizabeth to ensure that the plan of God for John would be implemented on the earth.

The first prophetic revelation of John begins with the Prophet Malachi.

"Behold, I am going to send My messenger, and he will clear the way before Me. And the Lord, whom you see will suddenly come to His temple…" (Malachi 3:1)

This prophecy speaks of John who was sent by God to prepare the way for Jesus. The only difference between the plan of God for John's life and the plan of God for your life is the manner in which He chose to keep John on track, which was accomplished through earlier prophecies and divine interventions.

Don't think for a minute that the angels sent to help you are not continually intervening in your life in much the same way. On the surface, it might not appear as radical for your life as others might, but the intentions of God toward you are every bit as important and necessary as anyone else born into the earth.

While I could easily take the opportunity to expound on other prophesies by Malachi in connection with John, as well as the words of Jesus speaking of John and Elijah, indicating they were one in the same, I will not. However, I will say that there is definitely more to "spirit" than we realize.

Much of Christianity seems to have this resolved conception of what spirit is; what it can do or not do, or who it can be or not be. When it comes to all of the possibilities within the realms of God's kingdom, we have barely skimmed the surface.

Everything in the earth is evolving, including our spiritual understanding. One truth leads to the next. I find it alarming when followers of Christ want to define scripture or spiritual experiences from a resolved perspective. Every new discovery is only one step to the next. Every spiritual revelation is merely the fringe of another infinite realm of eternity. I think most people, at least within the church, tend to bury their heads in the sand, refusing to look outside the box of traditional understanding. To assume that we have grasped or experienced the greater depths of God's word beyond basic revelation, in comparison to eternity and the knowledge therein, is a bit naïve, even arrogant.

Though John is not an isolated example, in many ways I think his birth breaks the theory of Adam and Jesus being the only ones to carry the life of the Spirit in such unique form.

Luke describes John's birth like this,

"For he will be great in the sight of the Lord; and he will drink no wine or liquor, and he will be filled with the Holy Spirit while yet in his mother's womb. And he will turn many of the sons of Israel back to the Lord their God. It is he who will go *as a forerunner* before Him in the spirit and power of Elijah, TO TURN THE HEARTS OF THE FATHERS BACK TO THE CHILDREN, and the disobedient to the attitude of the righteous, so as to make ready a people prepared for the Lord." (Luke 1:15-17)

This is an amazing account of God appearing to Zachariah telling him about the future birth of his son, John. Notice that John is described as one *"filled with the Holy Spirit while in his mother's womb."* This word "filled" means to be saturated with or completely under the influence of. It literally means that while John was still in his mother's womb he was completely under the influence of the mind of the Holy Spirit.

Therefore, the plan of God was already in his spiritual DNA, to such a degree, that John, like Jesus, would be born with an acute awareness of the intentions of God for his life. This is not to say that he would not have to grow up into this understanding and, like anyone else, have to make the right choices in life and be nurtured according to the will of God for his life. It was also said that John would *"go as a forerunner before Him (Jesus) in the spirit and power of Elijah."*

"In the spirit" speaks of the place, the spiritual realm, the spiritual heart and mind that John walked, which so happened to be the same realm, the same heart and mind that Elijah walked. John influenced the people much like Elijah did in his day in terms of turning the hearts of the people back to the fathers. Though both walked in the same influential realm of spiritual persuasion, they were, and still are, two different people. In heaven, both the spirit of Elijah and John exist as two separate beings with two separate personalities. In heaven you will have the opportunity to converse with each of them.

Notice how the Lord emphasizes to Zachariah that John would not "drink wine or liquor." This wasn't just an instruction for Zachariah and Elizabeth to follow concerning their son, this was a knowing that God put within the mind of John to ensure that John would walk in the ways of the Lord. I believe it was a condition required to keep John in the memory of God's plan for his life. Yes, I realize some of this was related to the priestly heritage that was on John, but the fact is there are potential experiences and exposures in a child's life that carry the ability to steer them off course. Revealing the plan of God to John's parents was another way of ensuring that John would be raised up in the way he was destined to go.

Lastly, I want to leave you with this thought concerning John. John's ability to recall God's intended purpose for his life was far more certain than most. This is not to say that other people are not as valued or loved as John, but our purpose in life varies. Therefore, depending on that purpose, the measures taken to ensure that the plans of God are carried out may vary as well. The birth of Jesus was dependent upon the fulfillment of prophecy, which included the birth and life of John preparing the way. This means that prior to being born in his mother's womb John knew in advance the significance of his birth and what it would mean for eternity. It is my prayer that while reading this book you would come into the realization of how much you are valued in the kingdom of God and the care that God has taken to ensure your earthly journey.

JESUS AND TOTAL RECALL

Jesus is our ultimate example of what it is like to walk in total recall of the Father's plan. I mean, come on. I know, some of you are thinking, "but He was Jesus, the Word, and God in the flesh." Yes, that is true, but the same Spirit that was working in Jesus is working in us right now. Like us, Jesus still had to resist temptation. He still had to learn what it was like to be obedient in the flesh.

"I glorified You on the earth, having accomplished the work which You have given Me to do. Now, Father, glorify Me together with Yourself, with the glory which I had with You before the world was." (John 17:4-5)

I have often marveled at the idea of Jesus being able to recall His previous glorious state prior to taking on the form of flesh on the earth. During the early years of His life, He grew up into the understanding that He was the Word, the son of God, destined to redeem the human race through His death and resurrection. He lived having full knowledge of previous prophecy and knew the importance of fulfilling each one. Jesus knew the plan of His Father in such detail that in the last days of His life on earth He was able to say, "...I glorified You on the earth, having accomplished the work which You have given Me to do."

Imagine what it would be like to know your purpose in life with such detail that when the moment of its fulfillment had come you would be able to say, *'Father I have accomplished the work you have sent me to do, now glorify me with the same glory that I had before I entered into this world.'*

I hope you can see this. The fact that you are "spirit" is proof that your origin is from the bosom of the Father. When the blood of Jesus redeemed you and me, that same redemption brought us into the awareness of our sonship in the Father. Through Jesus, the restorative process was initiated, which includes the restoration of memory, which was lost as the result of sin and everyday exposure to the conditions of a natural world.

Unlike the rest of the world, Jesus did not give into the temptations of the flesh. He submitted Himself to the will of the Father in all things. He maintained His perfected state at every level. He manifested a pure life to such a degree that all of His memories of his previous state of glory remained guarded and intact. Through Jesus, we have the ability to fix our minds on things above not on things below.

Thus the words of Paul,

"Therefore if you have been raised up with Christ, keep seeking the things above, where Christ is, seated at the right hand of God. Set your mind on the things above, not on the things that are on earth. For you have died and your life is hidden with Christ in God. When Christ, who is our life, is revealed, then you also will be revealed with Him in glory." (Colossians 3:1-4)

Wow! How wonderful is this? The fact that we have been raised with Christ places us in position of seeing things, eternal things, the way Jesus and the Father see them. Therefore, by setting my mind on things above, not on things on the earth, the life that I now live, hidden with Christ in God, reveals to me the hidden glory that had been in me even before the foundation of the world.

I can see clearly now, sitting with Christ and the Father saying, *"Wow, what a great view you have up here in this eternal place of Glory. Look, Father! That realm of glory over there is where I was standing when You came to me, giving me the opportunity to go into the earth as an ambassador of Your loving kindness."*

Ok. It's time for another "recall" exercise. Just say these words aloud:

"Father, thank You for giving me the best view in the house. Thank You for raising me up with Jesus so I can get a clear view of my glorious state in you. Father, thank You for reminding me of Your eternal intentions for my life."

Come on, take your time, and let this revelation soak into your spirit. It's time to decide, how much of the mind of Christ can we walk in? How much of His love and power can we exhibit in this generation? How much of His supernatural character can we take on? How much of the Father's plan for our life can we remember? What is the extent of our eternal recall? I say, *"Jesus had total recall. Why not me? Why not you?"*

"By this, love is perfected with us, so that we may have confidence in the Day of Judgment; because as He is, so also are we in this world." (1John 4:17)

MEMORY OF SOUL AND SPIRIT

In an effort to reach those who are not quite convinced of their eternal existence prior to entering into the earth in bodily form, I think it is necessary to briefly revisit our understanding of soul and spirit.

We know that God is Spirit; therefore, he is the source of all that is. When God formed man from the dust of the ground, He breathed into his nostrils the breath (spirit) of life; and man became a living being. (Genesis 2:7)

Imagine a man being formed out of the ground before actually becoming a living being. All you would have is a lifeless corpse. Without the breath of life there is no life, nothing is functional. All of the inward parts, the heart, mind, everything that pertains to that body is lifeless. Now imagine the breath of God coming into that lifeless form. You now have a body whose parts are completely functional and ***intelligent.*** This means the breath of God, is not just life, but also an intelligent force of energy. I realize this is a no brainer. I mean how could life come into these bodies without some kind of supernatural intelligence being the instigator? I realize there are many teachings out there that like to slice and dice the soul into multiple parts, but to a Hebraic person, the soul is the whole person. It is the unity of the body, breath and mind.

The most accurate meaning of the word "soul" is the Hebrew word "nephesh." It's not just some spiritual immaterial presence, it's all of you, your whole being. Today's revivalist will use the term "souls" in many ways to identify any number of people coming into revelation knowledge of Jesus Christ. This is because in their minds, a soul is the whole person.

Another thing we know about the body and soul is that when the body dies, the breath (spirit) returns to God. (Proverbs 20:27) I want to reemphasize that by mere definition alone, soul includes spirit, heart, mind and body. It's the whole enchilada. With that in mind, let's take a quick look at "spirit."

When the first man and woman disobeyed God in the Garden of Eden, they did not lose the breath or spirit of God, as some might believe. We know this because they did not drop dead. We have already established that the body cannot live without the life of the spirit. However, they did lose access to the tree of life. This meant they would eventually die, which the Lord told them would happen if they ate of the tree of knowledge of good and evil. This new knowledge created a self-awareness to such a degree that they slowly began to *forget* their former state of glory. In some ways, you might say they went stupid.

Through this one act of disobedience, the sin nature produced a spiritual amnesia, reducing humanity to mere flesh.

The writer of Genesis describes it like this,

"Then the LORD said, "My Spirit shall not strive with man forever, because he is also flesh"

A more accurate description of "strive" is "rule in." Some ancient versions read, "abide in."

In other words, *'My Spirit will not rule in man forever, because he has given himself over to the desires of the flesh.'* Like I said, stupid can appear in many ways.

Here we can see the final stage of the spirit of God diminishing to such an extent that humanity has now totally lost consciousness of its once glorious state. It's important to note that while someone can have the Spirit of God in them, *it is not the same has having the Spirit of God rule in them.*

The writer of Genesis then finalizes the intent of God with these words,

"Then the LORD saw that the wickedness of man was great on the earth, and that every intent of the thoughts of his heart was only evil continually." (Genesis 6:5)

This was a heartbreaking way of saying, *'they have totally forgotten Me. Every intention in their hearts is empty and void of anything that remotely looks like Me.'*

Of course, we know the salvation of a new beginning came through one human being, Noah, who found grace in the eyes of the Lord because he had not *forgotten.* I am so thankful Noah did not forget. The Spirit of God was still ruling in his heart and mind. In the eyes of God, a mature spiritual man or woman is one in whom the Spirit of God rules. Wherever the Spirit of the Lord is not ruling, the flesh is, and stupid is. Paul describes it like this,

"And I, brethren, could not speak to you as to spiritual men, but as to men of flesh, as to infants in Christ." (1Corinthians 3:1)

I intentionally took you the long way around to refresh your memory on the soul and spirit, how a human being can easily forget who he/she is in God, when the Spirit of God is not ruling in them and, in addition, the difference of the breath of God sustaining life, versus the Spirit of God ruling in that life. You would be amazed at the number of people who are not aware that spirit can hear, see, feel, smell, taste and touch. There are just as many who do not believe that you can hear, see, feel, or taste spirit. As I mentioned earlier, many believe that "spirit" is only a source of power, like a battery in a remote-controlled car; it is that, but yet so much more.

The most common Hebrew word translated for spirit is "ru' ahh" or another form of the same word is, "ruwach."

In the days of Noah, after the waters had covered the earth for a period of 150 days, God caused a wind to pass over the earth and the water subsided. **(Genesis 8:1)**

The word "wind" (ruwach) in this passage of scripture is the same word used for spirit, which you can feel and hear. Anytime "spirit" is presented like this you know you are in sync with its true meaning. This same wind (spirit) can be the wind blowing across a land, or it can be the wind of God.

67

David writes,

"By the word of the LORD the heavens were made, and by the breath of His mouth all their host." (Psalm 33:6)

Here we can see that "spirit" is able to create the heavens and host of armies.

Lastly, Zechariah the prophet declares,

"The oracle of the word of the LORD concerning Israel." " *Thus* declares the LORD who stretches out the heavens, lays the foundation of the earth, and forms the spirit of man within him..." (Zechariah 12:1)

Notice how the Spirit of God, the breath of God, the wind of God can move at any level, in any way it so chooses. It can blow across the earth and create unusual movement. It can divide the earth or bring it together. It can create something out of nothing. *It can even take on form and become a man within a man.*

It is this spirit of a man who has the power to recall a world outside of time. This same "wind" of God is the "breath," the guiding force within you and me. Many times in my ministry, I have prophesied to the man within the man. I have spoken to the spirit of the man that was before this time. There is the person of the spirit within the one in whom the Lord abides.

There is the other you, the spirit you, and yes, at the beckoning of the Spirit, it is able to leave your physical body. Through the prompting of the Holy Spirit, you can travel the universe. You can engage with other forms of creation or other spiritual beings in heaven. You can do all this while your physical body remains alive on earth. This and so much more is part of the predestined design of God for your life. The spirit of religion has taken our endless potential in God and reduced it to a human colony that can only engage with the realms of God's kingdom after it is dead. Come on. Really?

"*What* then if you see the Son of Man ascending to where He was before? [63] It is the Spirit who gives life; the flesh profits nothing; the words that I have spoken to you are spirit and are life." (John 6:62-63)

NATURAL AND SPIRITUAL MIND

Currently today, there are thousands of testimonies of men and women, young and old, who are having out-of-body experiences and going to heaven. Without fail, among many other things, all of these heavenly encounters reveal one important fact, and that is the spirit of man is a real, live, intelligent being whose origin is from above, not from below.

When the spirit of man separates from its earthly form, it has an intelligence that is beyond the human brain. Therefore, we can say there are seemingly two minds at work, one of the flesh and one of the spirit. However, it is the will of the Spirit to lead us into one mind, which is the mind of Christ.

The object of our journey on the earth is for the mind of the soul and body to come under the influence of the mind of the spirit, which is the Spirit of God living within these earthen vessels. The mind of the spirit is where the power of "recall" resides, thus bringing our souls into remembrance of the intentions of God for our lives.

While the natural mind can manifest a high measure of intelligence and accomplish many things, it is extremely handicapped without the influence of the other you, the spirit you, which by the way, is able to cross over into other dimensions in the twinkling of an eye. Much of the scientific community states that the majority of the human race uses a small percentage of its physical brain. However, humans have an unlimited capacity to learn. Unlike computers, no human brain has ever said, "my hard drive is full." The amount of brainpower being used at any given moment, compared to an infinite amount of potential, still leaves you with a small percentage of usage no matter how you slice it.

Since the spirit of man has a level of intelligence that is not of this world, its influence over the natural mind has the ability to increase its

71

learning capacity exponentially. The spirit, soul, and body were created to form a unique marriage in the kingdom of God. Yet, the physical mind and body are temporal vessels, temporary temples of the Holy Spirit to carry out the will of the Father on earth.

I'm reminded of a recent time of worship at MTI. During this particular worship gathering, I started singing about the temple of the Lord. What started out as a familiar image of our bodies being the temple of the Lord turned into something quite different. In that moment, I suddenly realized that apart from the natural mind and body, the soul and spirit of that same man is the eternal temple of the Lord. In other words, when we shed this natural body, the temple of the Lord is still intact.

This reminds me of another instance in Mary Neal's book, *"To Heaven and Back"* where she describes the emotion she felt after her body was being pulled out of the kayak by the force of the water. She speaks about the feeling of her soul being peeled away from her body. Then she describes a moment of total separation.

She writes,

"I felt a "pop." It felt as if I had finally shaken off my heavy outer layer, freeing my soul. I rose up and out of the river, and when my soul broke through the surface of the water, I encountered a group of fifteen to twenty souls (human spirits sent by God), who greeted me with the most overwhelming joy I have ever experienced and could ever imagine."

Shortly thereafter, Mary describes another moment when she glanced back at the scene of her lifeless body.

She writes,

"My body looked like the shell of a comfortable friend, and I felt warm compassion and gratitude for its use."

Notice the change? What was once the temple of life is no more. Nonetheless, the temple of the Lord continues on, but just in another form.

Right now, as I write these words, hundreds if not thousands of people all over the world are experiencing what it is like for their spirits and souls to leave their bodies. In that moment of separation, if they did not know it already, they will become completely aware of the intended plans of God for their lives. They will know what

73

they were sent into the world to do and how much of that plan was achieved. Of course, most of all, they will primarily be aware of the fathomless love of God.

However, the awesome news is you do not have to wait until your soul and spirit peel off your body before knowing what you were sent into this world to accomplish or to experience the awesome love of God. It could be that God wanted you to learn some things that pertain to love, gentleness, and kindness. Maybe, like John, you were sent to accomplish a particular mission to set the scene for the next revelation of heaven on earth. On the other hand, maybe you were sent here to help someone else achieve the destined purpose for his or her life. As you can see, the list for purpose is virtually endless.

May I remind you? You are destined to remember. You are destined to recall why you are here. The spirit of God in you already knows, but the transfer of information has yet to enter into your soul. It has yet to surface into the consciousness of your being.

It's time for another "recall" exercise. Please speak these words aloud.

"Holy Spirit, I realize that the spirit in me knows the intended purpose of my Father for my life. I do not want to leave this earth before fulfilling that very purpose. Holy Spirit, I ask You to help me transfer this foreknown knowledge into my soul, into the consciousness of my being."

Come on God!

The separation that Mary felt when her soul and spirit left her body is not the same experience when your spirit encounters heaven, or some other realm of God's kingdom.

This means that the Spirit of the Lord can take you on an amazing adventure at any given moment; all the while, your soul and body remain completely alive on earth.

Maybe the question should be asked, "How is it possible for the spirit to leave the body?" In order for this to happen, there has to be some sort of link between our spirit and God. This means that the Spirit of God in us is not ours, but His.

It also means that when our spirits leave our bodies we take on another form, one that is not made of flesh and blood. Again, I am not talking about the new body we receive after we shed off the old; that is the act of a final transformation. I am speaking of a spirit that has form and body, but of another realm.

Paul describes it like this,

"I know a man in Christ who fourteen years ago—whether in the body I do not know, or out of the body I do not know, God knows—such a man was caught up to the third heaven. And I know how such a man—whether in the body or apart from the body I do not know, God knows— was caught up into Paradise and heard inexpressible words, which a man is not permitted to speak." (2Corithians 12:2-4)

Notice how Paul repeatedly says, (paraphrase) "whether I was in my body or out of my body, I do not know…"

The only way you cannot know whether you are in your body or out of your body is to still have a body, to have form.

"I do know that I was caught up into another realm called Paradise and heard inexpressible words."

Paul realized that he had entered into another realm called "Paradise" where the knowledge there was inexpressible. This undoubtedly is a clear picture that the Spirit of God in us is a living being that is capable of functioning outside this natural body. It also means that this same spirit being has an intellect that is beyond the natural realm, which means it has a mind that is not of this world, thus capable of carrying memories of its former state.

UNIQUELY YOU

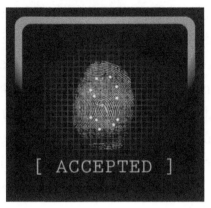

[ACCEPTED]

As I stated at the beginning of this book, memory is a natural part of God's design for all creation. Even an ant has enough memory to return to its home after it has ventured away to perform its daily tasks.

It's a scientific fact that at the moment of conception, there is an unusual force of energy that encompasses the embryo. Of course, we know that this mysterious source of energy is nothing less than the Spirit of God giving life to the seed of the womb. In the scientific world, it is stated that from the moment of conception, 46 chromosomes combined with 30,000 genes determine all of your physical characteristics; sex, facial features, body type and the color of your hair, eyes, and skin. Even more amazing, intelligence and personality - the way you think and feel, your talents, tastes, athletic abilities and more - were already in place within your genetic code. However, as great as this genetic coding is, it does not negate the fact that all of these physical characteristics are designed to operate under the influence of the mind of the spirit, which comes from God. Nonetheless, at the moment of conception, you were already essentially and uniquely 'you' - no bigger than a grain of sugar. I would also like to add that this "unique you" includes "the you" that is not of this world.

As mentioned before, at this stage of conception and then birth, you are more aware of the intentions of God for your life than any other period of human existence. You were born a good and excellent child. You were born amazing. However, once exposed to the physical world, without proper parental training you slowly began to forget who you are.

That is why I say, *"life is more about remembering what you forgot than learning what you never knew."*

Robin Sharma is one of the world's highly respected leadership experts. Over the years he has written several successful books. One of his books, a New York Times bestseller, *"The Leader Who Had No Title"* speaks about the art of remembering the real you, which he believes is one of the keys to becoming a great leader.

In his book, Robin describes a great leader not as someone becoming a better person, but seeing the perfection that is already in them.

Robin writes,

"The real mission is about remembering rather than improving."

He continues,

"Self leadership isn't about improving, because there's really nothing wrong with you. It's more about remembering. Remembering your inner leader and then making your relationship with it stronger each day. Self leadership has so much to do with simply reconnecting to the person you once were; to your true nature."

Robin continues to describe the importance of knowing who we were when we were little children.

"When we were young, society had not yet taught us how to deny our dreams, stifle our genius and smother our passion. Back then you weren't afraid to take some risks, learn new things, and

be completely comfortable to be exactly who you are."

I think Robin is on to something. While he might not openly accredit the real you as the "spirit you" or the true you as the one foreknown by God, he certainly has enough understanding to know that the real genius in each of us, while still very young, is either suppressed, devalued and misunderstood, or nurtured and encouraged to its fullest potential.

His overall assessment is to *"live life backward."* Instead of trying to become great, see how great you already are and how great you already were.

Here is an amazing man who lays claim to his ability to recall or remember the original intent for his life. As a result, directly influencing the leadership at Microsoft, GE, FedEx, IBM, Nike, NASA and Yale University just to name a few.

The power of restoration entails so many things in life, including bringing to our remembrance what our purpose is as sons/daughters in the kingdom of God. Who would have thought that when Jesus arrived on the scene that through His death and resurrection, a veil of forgetfulness would be removed from our minds, thus enabling us to see the original intent of heaven in us.

MEMORY IN THE BLOOD

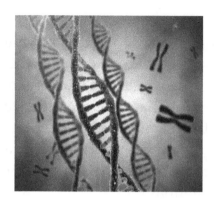

For most of my teenage years, I lived a very reckless life. I was always pushing things to the limit. In my home town of Dryden, WA riding motorcycles, snowmobiles and any other off road vehicle was a normal part of transportation, whether to school and back or just for personal enjoyment. Hardly a year would pass without me encountering some sort of accident, which usually resulted in multiple broken bones or concussions. Talk about a lapse in memory, it's a miracle that I am graced with the heart and mind that I have today.

Because of my reckless teen years, it was discovered in 1998 that a golf-ball sized cyst had formed on the frontal lobe of my brain, which was said to be the result of a number of concussions that I had acquired years earlier. After the cyst was removed, I was anxious to move on with my life no longer having to deal with the focal seizures that had previously been the result of this growth. A few weeks after the surgery, the seizures started up again. I remember how shocked and disappointed I was thinking this nightmare in my life was still not over. I immediately called the surgeon wanting to know why I was still having these awful seizures.

He said, *"Even though the cyst has been removed, the memory of your brain is still acting as though you never had the surgery. Stay in the mind that this has been removed and the symptoms should subside in the near future."*

After speaking with the surgeon, I made a decision not to take any more medication and stood in faith, believing that it was over. A short time later, the seizures stopped never to return again. I guess you might say it was a type of phantom limb pain, which is what a person feels after the loss of a limb. At the most basic core of our being, memory is said to be in our blood. It is otherwise known as "cellular memory." Cellular memory is the hypothesis that such things as memories, habits, interests, and tastes may somehow be stored in all the cells of human bodies, not only in the brain.

On May 29, 1988, a woman named Claire Sylvia received the heart of an 18-year-old male who had been killed in a motorcycle accident. Soon after the operation, Sylvia noticed some distinct changes in her attitudes, habits, and tastes. She found herself acting more masculine, strutting down the street (which, being a dancer was not her usual manner of walking). She began craving foods such as green peppers and beer, which she had always disliked before. Sylvia even began having recurring dreams about a mystery man named Tim L., who she had a feeling was her donor. As it turns out, he was. Upon meeting the "family of her heart," as she put it, Sylvia discovered that her donor's name was, in fact, Tim L., and that all the changes she had been experiencing in her attitudes, tastes, and habits closely mirrored that of Tim's.

While some might find this a bit unnerving, maybe even spooky, I find it to be in perfect harmony with the design of God. The memory of our natural state mirrors the memory of our spirit. Memory of the spirit is in our blood. Every cell carries the revelation of our state prior to earth. Think about this, the blood of Jesus flows through our veins. His redemptive power has made it so. We were born to recall, not just the natural things in life, but the things of the spirit as well. What an amazing revelation of both memory and life in the blood.

Ok. Here we are. Time for another "recall" exercise.

"Help me Lord to forget the things that need to be forgotten and to remember the things that need to be remembered. Thank you for creating this body with the ability to remember and for giving me a spirit that has the power to do the same."

THE PLANNING ROOM

Paul writes,

"Therefore if you have been raised up with Christ, keep seeking the things above, where Christ is, seated at the right hand of God. Set your mind on the things above, not on the things that are on earth. For you have died and your life is hidden with Christ in God." (Colossians 3:1-3)

These passages of scripture are far more meaningful in my life today than years past. The idea that we have been lifted up in Christ, into the same realm of glory, seated at the right hand of God, is the ultimate revelation of the endless access that is available to us. He has given us the ability to set our mind on things above, on the heavenly realm, so much so, that we are able to access the eternal realms of glory, which include the planning room of God.

Wow! Did I just say that? Yes, I did. There's a place in heaven where all the plans of God are created and put into motion. It's a very real place. The memory of this supernatural planning room is locked away in our spiritual DNA. The only question is, 'How do we tap into it?' Maybe you have wondered, 'what does such a place look like or sound like?' Well, let's peek in and see.

Jeremiah knew what it was like to encounter the preplanned purpose of God for his life.

"Before I formed you in the womb I knew you, and before you were born I consecrated you; I have appointed you a prophet to the nations." (Jeremiah 1:5)

Many of you have heard someone quote this passage of scripture or have read it for yourself multiple times. I think the implications behind this verse are astounding in terms of our interaction with God as spiritual beings, prior to being born on the earth.

"Knew" comes from the Hebrew "yada" which means to know. It literally means *"to be acquainted with or to instruct."* No matter how you slice it, Jeremiah was interacting with God up

close and personal before he entered his mother's womb. This wasn't just some image or thought in God's mind. During this time of instruction, it is noted that God set Jeremiah aside and appointed him a prophet to the nations. I know some of you are thinking, "That was Jeremiah, not me." Come on, really? It wasn't as if God preplanned the life of Jeremiah and no one else. Though the plan of God for your life is not spelled out in the Bible, it is however, recorded in heaven. Moreover, in heaven, the plans of God are available for everyone to read. Yes, that's right. In heaven, your missions in life are public knowledge. Everyone has the opportunity to not only view the design of God for your life, but they have access to your daily progress.

For the most part, prophets or any other individuals that operate with the gift of knowledge are able to speak about your future, in terms of God's purpose and plan for your life. By the spirit, they are accessing public information from heaven. They are hearing the recorded information concerning your life. I'm not implying every action you take on earth has been pre-recorded or predestined, but the major expectations of your journey have, and your decisions leading up to those moments of fulfillment are recorded as well. It's much like a game in motion. The individual plays are determined by the players in the game, which reveal the character and strategy of each player. However, in the end, the final score was already set from the foundations of the world. I have good news for you; you win because Jesus has already won. Nonetheless, you still have to be a willing participant to become a part of the winning team.

The fact that a prophet or any other prophetic individual is able to access the foreknown knowledge of God's purpose and destiny for your life is proof that your life, like Jeremiah, was set into motion before you were in your mother's womb.

Like Jeremiah, you are spirit from another world, another realm of glory. Yes, it's true, God knew you before you were in your mother's womb. He spoke over your life. He gave you divine instructions. In the beginning, He included you in the purpose and destiny for your life.

Still having trouble remembering? Well, so are many other people. However, like you, many others are on the threshold of remembering. A huge shift is about to take place. Millions of people are about to enter into a state of total recall. This is the revelation of the great awakening, not only to know who we are, here and now, but who we were always destined to be.

FOREKNOWN AND PREDESTINED

While we are on the subject, we might as well look deeper into the meaning of what it means to be foreknown or predestined. After all, it is linked to our ability to recall the plans of God for our life.

First, let me clear the air by saying, being foreknown or predestined does not mean that our future is robotically planned, it just means that each of us have a predestined course, which is subject to the daily choices in our life. My previous analogy of using GPS while driving would fit well here. The Holy Spirit is continually lovingly and patiently keeping us on track.

"And we know that all things work together for good to those who love God, to those who are called according to *His* purpose. For those whom He foreknew, He also predestined *to*

become conformed to the image of His Son, so that He would be the firstborn among many brethren; and these whom He predestined, He also called; and these whom He called, He also justified; and these whom He justified, He also glorified." (Romans 8:28-30)

There are a few things to consider in these passages of scripture. First, let's look at the definition of "foreknew" and "predestined", their meaning, and how they differ from one another.

Foreknew is the Greek word "**pro**ginosko" which means to "know beforehand or to foresee." It is derived from the root Greek word "pro" which means "to be in front of, or prior to." The implications behind these definitions carry the weight of superiority. This tells us that the predestined purposes of God for our life are superior to anything else. It also implies that this foreknown knowledge was placed in front of, given to us or planned out, prior to anything else, which includes our entrance in the earth.

These two definitions present an interesting combination of meaning. God *foreknew* us, meaning he knew his intentions toward us, in advance. It also means that he *pre-selected* us for a specific purpose. God *foresaw* us in the future and predetermined the ultimate course for our life. None of which would be possible without prior personal interjection with us before, and after entering our mother's womb.

If you remember, (no pun intended) in the previous chapter *"The past and the future"* I presented to you a different view about the past and the future.

I wrote,

"From a Hebraic perspective, what is visible is "in front of" and what is invisible "is behind." In this sense, the past is the future and the future is the past."

It's no coincidence that the word, "foreknew" follows the same meaning "in front of, or prior to" which implies that the knowledge of your purpose in life, your future, was pre-known or predetermined before time.

Predestination

Predestined, comes from the Greek word, *"proorizo"* which means to *"limit in advance or to predetermine."* It comes from the same root word, "pro" meaning in front of, or prior to."

I think the best way to sum up this chapter is by highlighting the word, *"limit."*

Job describes "limit" like this,

"You put my feet in the stocks and watch all my paths; You set a limit for the soles of my feet..." (Job 13:27)

At first glance, it might appear as if God is some heavy task master strapping Job to a ball and chain preventing him from going anywhere in life. Given Job's situation, I'm sure there were moments when Job felt like he was being cast into the dungeon of forgetfulness and the key thrown away.

Yet, all of this is really another way of saying, 'you have predetermined the course of my life.' Job is articulating the fact that God has restricted him from walking down any other path except the one designed for him. Thus his words, "you set a limit for the soles of my feet." This is not to say that God was forcing Job's hand, but knowing the heart of Job and his relationship with the Lord, in Job's mind, his only recourse was to lay down his life and trust God to the very end.

The Hebrew word for "limit" is "carve" which means the Lord carved out the life of Job in advance. Again, this is not a picture of God usurping the will of Job, but the reality of the influence that God had in Job's life. Like anyone else, Job had the opportunity to choose another path, but chose the way of the Lord.

Lastly, before moving on to the next chapter, I want to leave you with this final thought. God was the one that provoked Satan to challenge Job's dedication.

"The LORD said to Satan, "Have you considered My servant Job? For there is no one like him on the earth, a blameless and upright man, fearing God and turning away from evil." (Job 1:8)

Given the fact that God is the one who rarely acts on sudden impulse, if at all, in terms of the future, this is a strong indication that Job knew in his heart that this was his predestined purpose in life. It was in his spiritual genes to stand against all odds. Do I believe Job had a moment of "total recall?" Possibly, but whatever the case, the life of Job was sculptured out, in advance, before time.

REMEMBERING THROUGH CREATIVITY

In these final chapters I am going to show you *"how to"* recall, not just the plans of God for your life, but any other experience that you might have had in heaven or any other kingdom realm of God. Yes, I know it might sound "too good to be true" but as my dear mother used to say, (who has gone to be with the Lord) "the proof of the pudding is in the eating."

A few years back, Lori and I and a few other close friends were invited to Akiane Kramarik's home. Akiane is primarily a self-taught painter. She is a young prodigy that claims that God spoke to her when she was three years old, encouraging her to paint and draw her visions. Her parents were atheists at the time. They later converted to Christianity because of Akiane's paintings and visions. Akiane started drawing at the age of four, advancing to painting at six, and writing poetry at seven. Her first completed self-portrait sold for $10,000. According to Akiane, her art is inspired by her visions of heaven, and her personal connection with God. Her art depicts life, landscape, and people. She is presently one of the world's leading realistic painters.

During our visit, the family took us on a tour of her paintings, which they had displayed throughout their house upstairs and down. While there, we learned that Akiane really didn't know what she was going to paint until she started painting. We were told that it wasn't until after she had started painting that she would have extreme moments of total recall. During those times, she would remember a particular experience or vision that she had while in heaven.

I watched an earlier video of Katie Couric interviewing Akiane on CBS. During this interview, Akiane tells Katie that she lacked the vocabulary to describe her heavenly encounters, but she was able to express her visitation through color.

So, let's stop here for a moment and home in on something very important. One of the keys to recalling an event or gaining understanding that is not of this world is through the gateway of creativity.

Everyone has a creative side, because everyone has an imagination. With the power of imagination comes the power to create. No, you might not be an Akiane, but you have the ability to create something. The creative force of the spirit in you, by default, places you within the scope of recalling a side of your spiritual nature that is truly not of this world.

Most people have had glimpses of certain images or have had thoughts about things that do not add up in the physical world around them. Most people brush this off as being a figment of their imagination, a fantasy world that seems nothing more than make-believe. However, I want to suggest to you that many of those far-out images that have surfaced in your mind could very well be your spirit trying to jog your memory of a truth or experience that took place concerning purpose in life.

Come on now, stay with me. The Lord is going to demonstrate the life of the spirit that is behind these words and the power they have to stir the "other you" into spiritual awareness.

In this same interview, Akiane describes how she was only ten years old when she started painting **"Creation"** a well-known piece of art in her collection. She said it wasn't until after she started putting the brush to the canvas that she remembered her previous experience in heaven.

She states,

"The painting "Creation" actually came into being by accident. It was a time when I let myself go and somehow this image came about and I suddenly remembered that it was an actual place I used to visit as a child."

Oh man, let me tell you, I know what that is like. I know what it is a like to give myself completely over to the spontaneity of praise and worship and through my imagination suddenly find myself in another world. I know what it's like to travel through stars and galaxies. I've experienced the sensation of passing through the Milky Way, exploring the universe in ways unimaginable. Some might read this with disbelief, but many others will know exactly what I am talking about, because you have had the same experience. Maybe not with stars and galaxies, but possibly with color, sound, glorious images that look like nothing you have ever seen before.

I decree over you right now, "Remember! Remember the glory of heaven! Remember the Father's touch!"

I remember one of the first times when I prophesied about what creation would look like in the future. As I leaned into this intense word of knowledge, images that I had never seen before suddenly appeared in the spirit of my mind. I saw trees releasing light, and what looked like the dirt of the ground was so rich looking, I wanted to eat it. I saw walls made of light, walls that were keeping things out and other things in.

After this first encounter I thought, "Wow! The future is amazing!" I realized later that what I was seeing then was something I had already seen before. What was destined to be the future here on earth, already existed in heaven. *I remembered.* No, this is not always the case, but many times it is. As I've already stated, there is a thin line between the past, present and future. There is a thin line between learning something for the first time versus remembering what you already knew.

THE OTHER YOU

Another key to remembering, is tapping into the *"other you,"* which is awakened through the spirit of prophecy. The first time I came across this understanding was a number of years back when I did a study on the life of Saul. After Samuel had anointed Saul to become king of Israel, he told him about three men he would meet along the way. After encountering these men, Samuel instructed Saul to do the following,

"Afterward you will come to the hill of God where the Philistine garrison is; and it shall be as soon as you have come there to the city, that you will meet a group of prophets coming down from the high place with harp, tambourine, flute, and a lyre before them, and they will be prophesying.

6 Then the Spirit of the LORD will come upon you mightily, and you shall prophesy with them and be changed into another man."

During this study, I learned that being changed into *"another"* man really meant being changed into the *"other"* man. The other you is the real you, the one who is submitted to the influence of the Spirit. As soon as Saul was exposed to the spirit of prophecy he was transformed into the "other" Saul; the one destined to become the first king of Israel. I would also like to point out that prior to Saul discovering his other self, something happened to him when Samuel anointed him the king.

"Then it happened when he (Saul) turned his back to leave Samuel, God changed his heart; and all those signs came about on that day." (1 Samuel 10:9)

As soon as Samuel prophesied to Saul about the "other" Saul, God changed the heart of Saul, which set the stage for Samuel's prophecy to come to pass. Saul's encounters with Samuel offer us another key to remembering the plans and purposes of God for our own life, which come through the power of prophecy. When Saul encountered the prophet, thus the power of prophecy, another dimension of the Spirit of God

101

was revealed to him. This spiritual dimension dramatically altered the life of Saul. Saul's increasing exposure to the spirit of prophecy, first with Samuel, then the other prophets, revealed another man, the other Saul, the one fashioned by the Spirit.

This is a wonderful kingdom tip for walking in total recall. The spirit of prophecy has the potential to unlock all the secret chambers of your heart that carry the revelation knowledge of the "other you." This other life in you is the one that knows the pre-plans of God for your life. I cannot count the number of times when I have prophesied over individuals only to see them rise up into a supernatural awareness of their purpose and destiny in God, all of which was there all along, but hidden and forgotten.

There are amazing testimonies of men and women who have instantly recalled forgotten supernatural encounters they experienced in heaven while they were in their first few childhood years, or even before birth. Hard to believe? Then I challenge you to go to a place where the genuine presence of prophecy resides, *expecting* the Spirit of God to bring to your remembrance all things that are destined for you in this hour. You will be glad you did. I am reminded of a young man that I met while in ministry on the streets of Yakima a number of years ago. At the time, this man had the look of a homeless person. Yet when I looked at him, I didn't see a man without means, but a man who was sitting in a place of government. I told him about the great plans God had for his life, one of which was to put him in the seat of government.

Given his condition at the time, to others it sounded as though I was out of my mind, which was a true assessment, because I wasn't in my mind, but in the mind of the Spirit. Some years later, I received an email, via Facebook from this same man. He reminded me who he was and told me that he was now mayor of the city of Union Gap, Washington. I shouted, "God! You are amazing!" I didn't just see into his future, but by the Spirit of the Lord, I saw a portion of God's plan for his life, one that was given to him before time.

Time does not permit me to fully describe the power of influence that the spirit of prophecy has to awaken the soul of a man or woman. To see the future from heaven's past. To transcend time, accessing the planning chambers of glory, where countless lives are born out of the bosom of the Father, destined to reveal His heart and purpose throughout the earth. For almost 20 years, I have abandoned myself into this unique expression of prophetic utterance. Time after time, I have remembered my call in life. I have gained new understanding as to the intentions of God for humanity.

Through the spirit of prophecy, I have seen a new heaven and earth. I have engaged with glorious creatures that are not of this world, but are a part of the glory of God. One of the keys to remembrance is to set your mind on things above, not on things below. Our focus in life is everything. For too long now, many have focused on death rather than life, resulting in total amnesia instead of total recall.

The voice of our Father is calling throughout the earth, "Remember Me! Remember who you are! Remember where you come from! Remember my glory! Remember!" It is true, the Lord has commissioned each of us, like Jesus, to walk with total recall.

Ok. It's Time for another recall moment. Please read this aloud.

"Father, I know that I am destined to remember who I am and all that you have afforded me in this hour. Father, set me free from any blindness. Set me free from any spiritual amnesia that has plagued my heart and mind. Father, show me your glory! Like Jesus, show me the glory that I knew before this time."

MEDITATION AND IMAGINATION

In the mid 1980's, new age believers catapulted into a national movement. Since that time, they have dominated many spiritual practices, including meditation. Many people in the national media have been quoted as saying, *"The New Age Movement is the most powerful social force in the world today"*

While I am uncertain as to the accuracy of this statement, there is no doubt that new age believers make up a very large percentage of the world's social influence. Many believe the New Age Movement stole a large portion of their spiritual practices from the Christian community. I don't believe they stole anything. I think most in the Christian world just handed them over out of fear. Somewhere along the road, most Christian followers refused to associate with anything that remotely looked like, or sounded like "new age" practices.

As a result, the majority of Christians steer away from teachings that involve meditation and imagination. Still today, whenever I use those two words together in most Christian circles, I can feel the tension in the air. I do not believe this is about taking something back from some other spiritual movement; this is about bringing to your remembrance something that is still in you, something that was given to you before time. In the previous chapter, I briefly wrote about the power of imagination and its connection to creativity. I shared with you the power it has to give you total recall, as well as bring you into something fresh and new in the spirit. I would like to expound on that further, in conjunction with meditation, which is every bit as important and powerful.

Before I jump into the spiritual benefits of meditation and the use of imagination, I would like to mention briefly some amazing facts that science has discovered about meditation and its effect on the brain.

Through the observation of MRI scans, neuroscientists have learned that meditation strengthens the brain by reinforcing the connections between brain cells. A 2012 study showed that people who meditate exhibit higher levels of gyrification — the "folding" of the cerebral cortex as a result of growth, which in turn may allow the brain to process information faster. Though the research did not prove this directly, scientists suspect that gyrification is responsible for making the brain better at processing information, making decisions, forming memories, and improving attention.

Much of the research shows that meditation causes the brain to undergo physical changes, which are all very beneficial. Other studies have also shown that meditation is linked to cortical thickness, which can result in decreased sensitivity to pain.

A 2009 study that was given the title, "Long-term meditation", revealed increased gray matter density in the brain stem. Neuroscientists used MRIs to compare the brains of meditators with non-meditators. The structural differences observed led the scientists to speculate that certain benefits, like improved cognitive, emotional, and immune responses, can be tied to this growth and its positive effects on breathing and heart rate (cardio respiratory control).

It goes without saying that the list of positive effects that meditation has on the physical body as a whole are endless and well worth the research if you have a desire to increase your quality of life.

However, the spiritual potential of meditation, along with the harnessing of imagination, is even more remarkable and well worth the finding out.

The prophet Isaiah speaks about Isaac as being a man of meditation.

"Isaac went out to meditate in the field toward evening..." (Genesis 24:63)

The Hebrew word "meditate" means to "muse pensively. It means to think or meditate on a thought, subject, or place." One important aspect of Hebrew is that meditation is murmuring aloud your musings, to yourself, or to God. It is believed that it brings in the wonderful connection of the voice, because there can be no voice without the breath, (spirit). It is also believed that the spirit and soul join together to speak, which includes the body, for the physical breath has to pass through the vocal chords for a sound to be made. There is creative power in our voice. This could explain the 'rocking' motion of the Jewish prayer, which also involves the body being engaged and in unity with soul and spirit.

Multiple scriptures in the Bible depict David as a man of continual meditation.

David often meditated in his heart while lying on his bed. **(Psalms 4:4)**

David writes,

"I will remember my song in the night; I will meditate with my heart and my spirit ponders. (Psalms 77:6)

The word "ponders" means to search or to be searched. This implies that David was meditating with his heart, while the Spirit searched the depths of his heart.

God speaks to Solomon these words,

"As for you, my son Solomon, know the God of your father, and serve Him with a whole heart and a willing mind; for the LORD searches all

hearts, and understands every intent of the thoughts..." (1 Chronicles 28:9)

It also means that, by the Spirit, David was able to search the mysteries of God.

In reference to the things that God has prepared for those who love Him,

Paul writes,

"For to us God revealed *them* through the Spirit; for the Spirit searches all things, even the depths of God. For who among men knows the *thoughts* of a man except the spirit of the man which is in him? Even so the *thoughts* of God no one knows except the Spirit of God. Now we have received, not the spirit of the world, but the Spirit who is from God, so that we may know the things freely given to us by God..." (1Corithians 2:10-12)

There are two very important things to note here, "the spirit of the man" and the "Spirit of God." Outside of the Spirit of God, only your spirit can know your thoughts or intentions. However, with the Spirit of God we can know, not only the original us, but the mind of God for us. Which means, through the Spirit of God we can recall the preplanned intentions of God for our lives. The Spirit of God freely gives us all of this information and so much more.

Come on! This is amazing! Through the Spirit of God in us we can gain access to the mysteries of creation, the mysteries of the universe, the mysteries of heaven, and all else that is eternal.

For a man or woman of God, spiritual meditation is a means to gain access to multiple realms of God's kingdom.

A large portion of this Kingdom knowledge can be accessed through the practice of meditating on the Word of God, and by yielding your imagination to the Spirit. Divine meditation affords us the opportunity to focus on the purposes of God for our life. It enables us to regain any forgotten knowledge of who we are and who we are destined to be in the kingdom of God.

A few times now, I have referred to the phrase in scripture, *"set your mind,"* which implies setting your mind on things above. This was Paul's instruction to the Colossians in his day.

"...Set your mind on the things above, not on the things that are on earth..." (Colossians 3:1-4)

This is literally a call to meditate on heaven. To fix your heart and mind on a life that is not of this world. Every form of meditation requires imagination, which offers us the ability to dial into a supernatural realm called the *"throne of glory."* By meditating on this seat of glory, which is where we are right now in Christ, we are able to recall any information that is pertinent to our previous and current state in Him.

When was the last time you read the **"throne room encounters"** of John in the book of Revelation? When was the last time you took the time to meditate on these and other scriptural references that describe the glory of the Lord in great detail?

One of the avenues for experiencing one of the throne room realms of glory, (there are more than one) as described by Isaiah, Ezekiel and John, is through the meditation of the Word and your imagination.

I know from personal experience what it is like to access the kingdom realms of God through meditation and imagination.

ACCESSING THE SUPERNATURAL

On June 29, 2012, I was approaching the front door of our home when I tripped on the steps and fell hard on the concrete patio. The fall was severe enough that I had to have emergency care. During my visit to the emergency room at Regional Hospital, they x-rayed my wrist and called in a specialist to assess the injury.

They showed me the x-rays, which revealed two fractures, one on the top of my wrist at the radius and ulna, and one on the side of the wrist, at the lunate and tri-quetrum. My daughter, who is a registered nurse, was working in the emergency department at the time of my accident. She was also present when the x-rays were being viewed. After putting me in a cast, I was scheduled to go see a specialist on July 3, 2012 to determine the proper course of care for this particular kind of fracture.

On the morning of my appointment, I awoke early in the morning to spend some time in meditation with the Lord. During my time of meditation, I remember setting my mind on the glory of the Lord. I envisioned His throne in heaven and all the activity around it as described by John and others in scripture.

After a while, in my imagination, or in the spirit of my mind, I saw what appeared to be an old clay oven with burning fire in it. I instantly felt compelled to put my hand into it, which I did. It felt very hot, but not so hot that I could not stand it.

I remember putting my hand in and out of the fire, when all of a sudden I found myself standing between two walls of blue flames burning on either side of me. Between these two walls of fire there was a path made of gem-like stones beneath my feet. As I walked down the path, I was compelled to stretch out my arms and run them through the burning flames. When I did, I was surprised to find that the flames were cold instead of hot like the previous fire.

I then became aware of the time and realized that I was running late for my doctor's appointment. To make a long story short, the orthopedic doctor had his assistant remove my cast and take new x-rays of my fractured wrist.

A short time later, the doctor showed me the x-rays on the overhead viewing screen.
He said,

"The x-rays on the left are the ones that were taken at the time of your injury and the x-rays on the right are the ones we just now took. As you can see the fractures appear to be very evident on the left, but the x-rays on the right show very little sign of any fracture at all."

Of course, the doctor and I had to do a little arm wrestling as to the reason for this dramatic change in my wrist. At the end of my visit, he was still reluctant to place the outcome of this injury in the category of a miracle.

As I walked away from the orthopedic surgeon, I knew without a doubt that the experience I had a few hours earlier, was indeed a very real supernatural experience.

I have since become a strong believer in the power of meditation and I continually set my mind and my imagination on things above and not on things below.

Finally, brethren, whatever things are true, whatever things are noble, whatever things are just, whatever things are pure, whatever things are lovely, whatever things are of good report, if

there is any virtue and if there is anything praiseworthy — *meditate on these things.* (Philippians 4:8)

Now for our final "recall" exercise:

"Father, I acknowledge that the Holy Spirit, whom You gave to me, resides within me. Therefore, through the practice of spiritual meditation, and through the yielding of my imagination, I ask You to reveal to me the mysteries of creation, of heaven, and of eternity. Father, show me everything that is pertinent to my divine journey on earth."

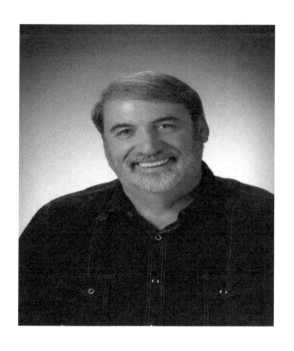

To order other books and materials by

Michael A. Danforth.

Please log on to our website at:

www.mticenter.com
Or
You can write to
MTI
PO Box 43
Yakima, WA. 98907